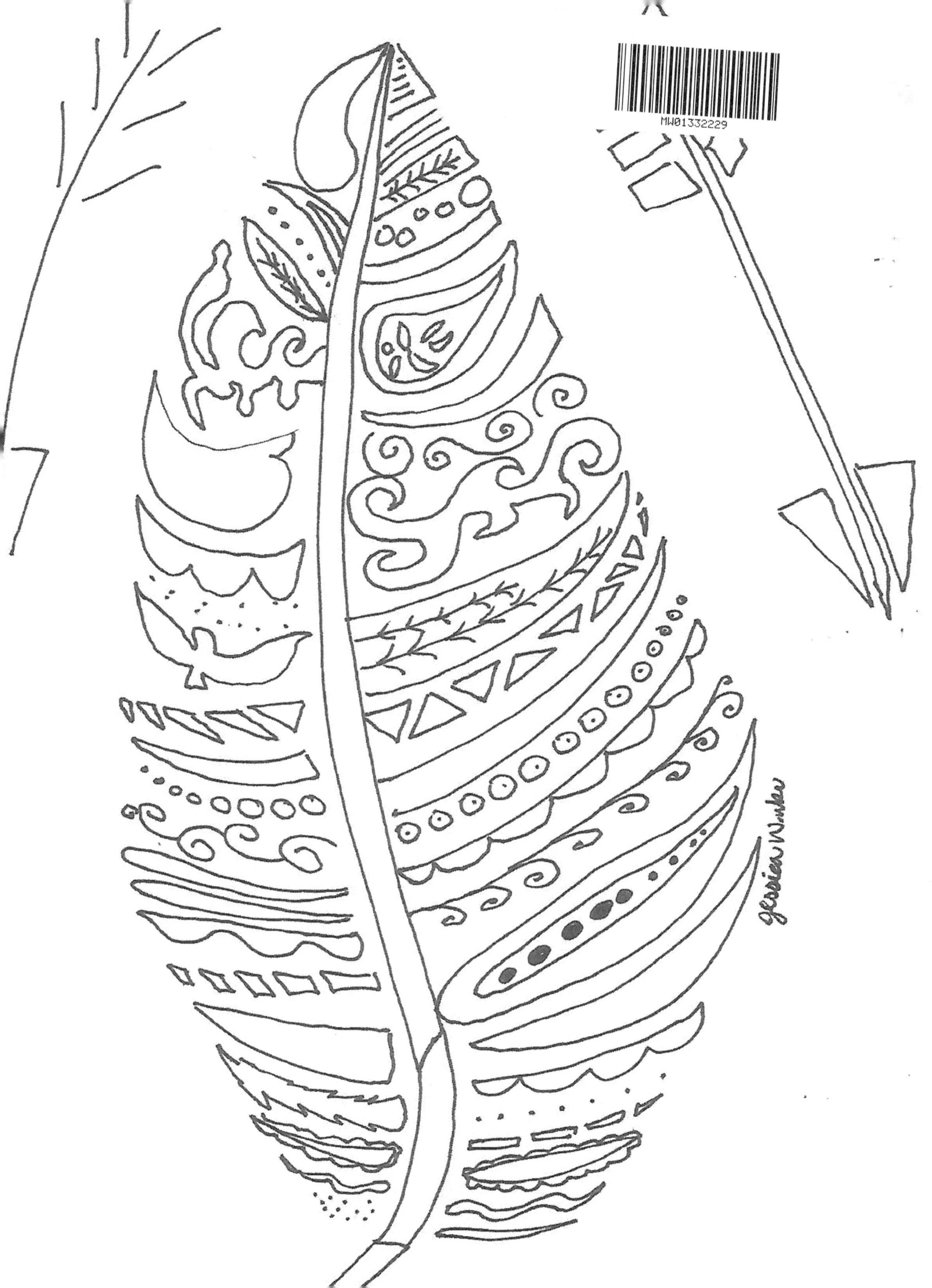

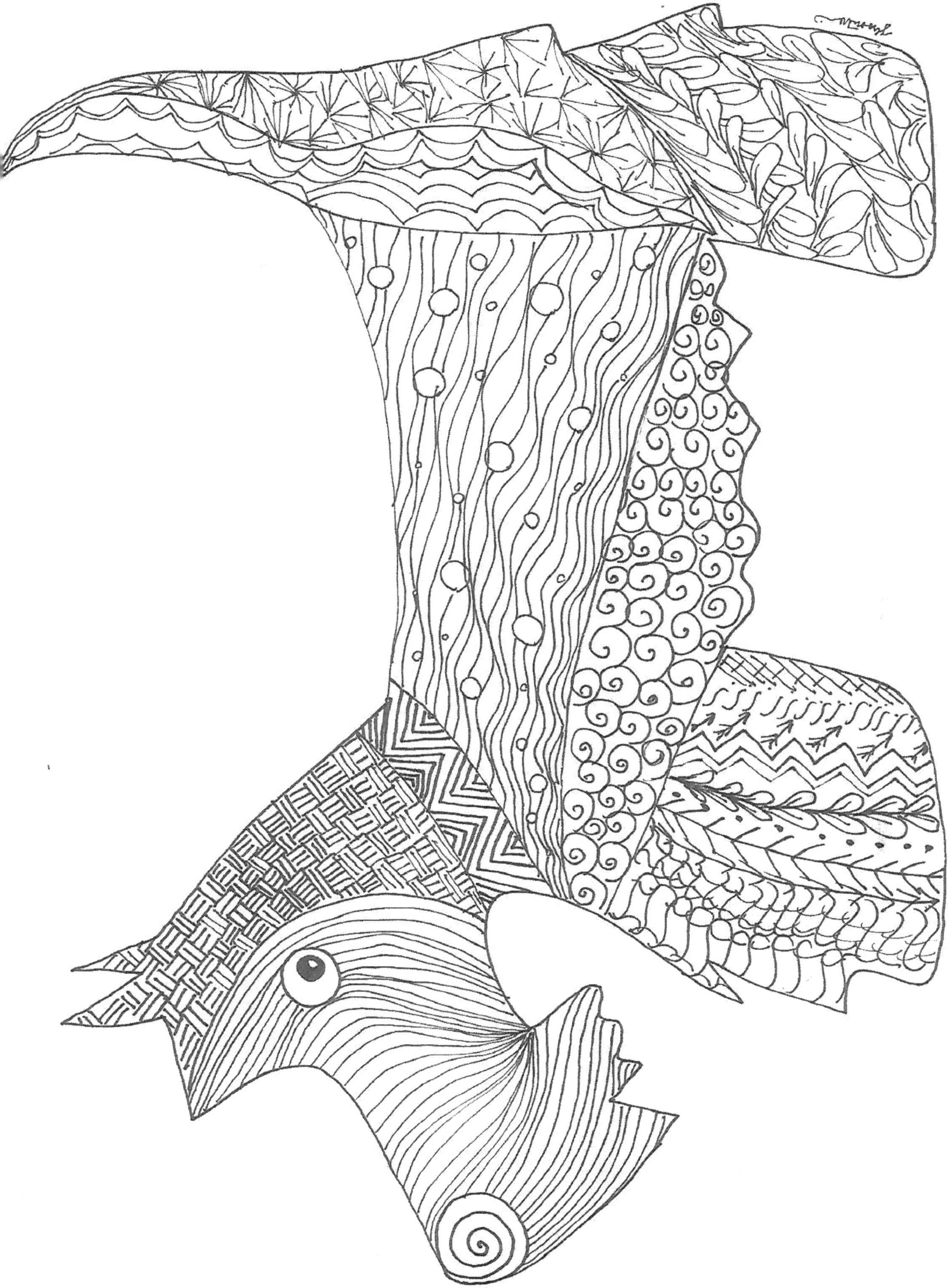

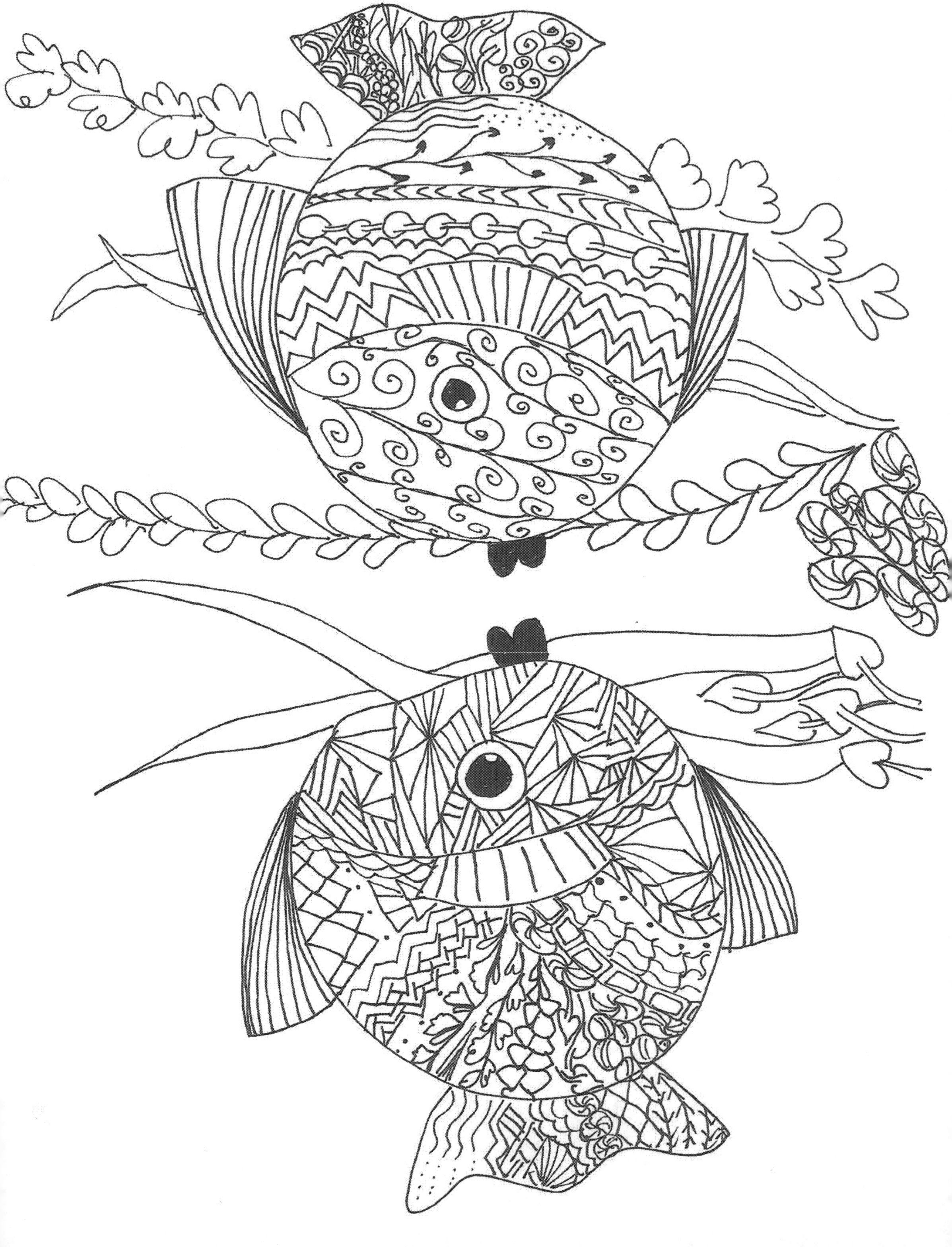

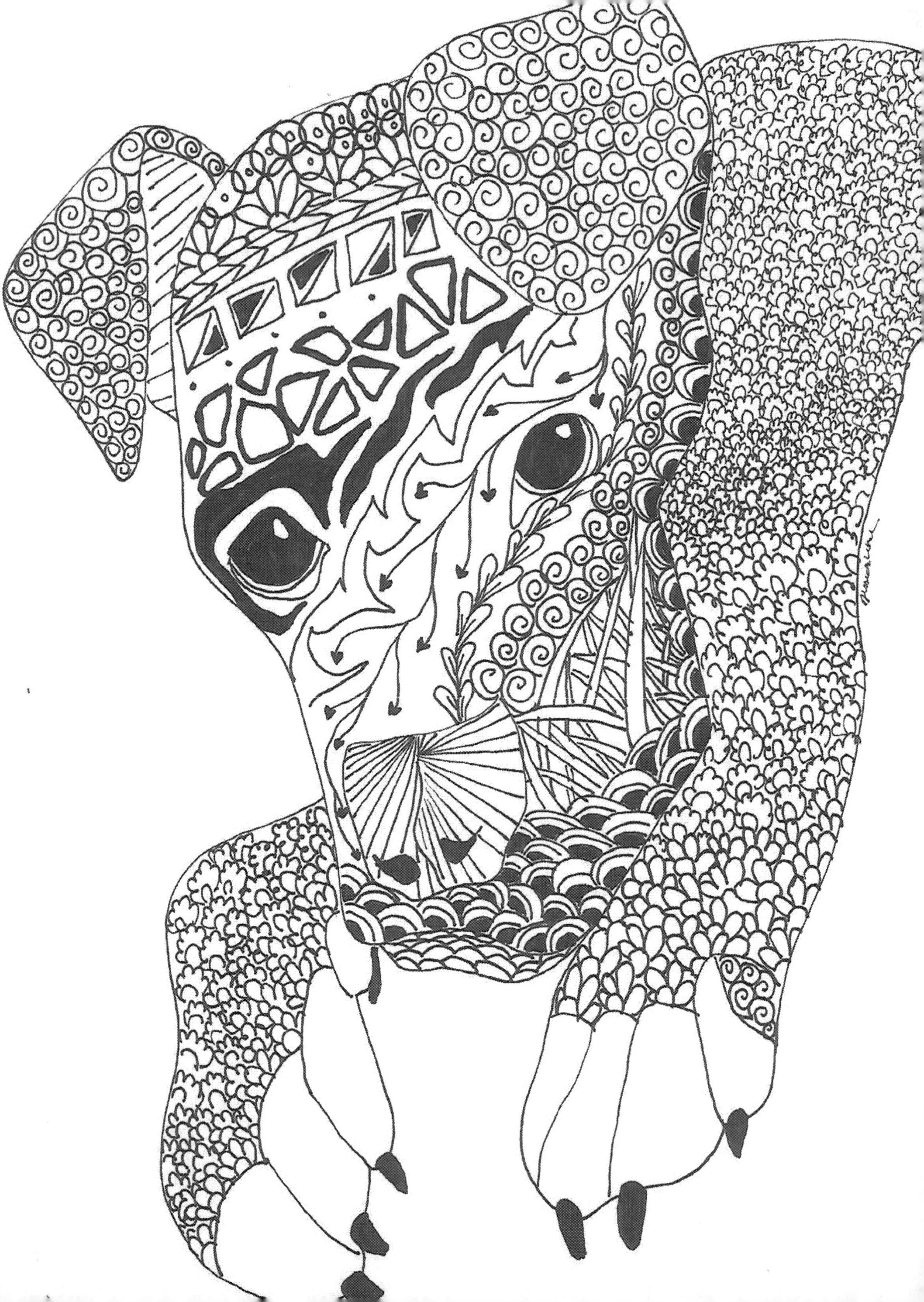

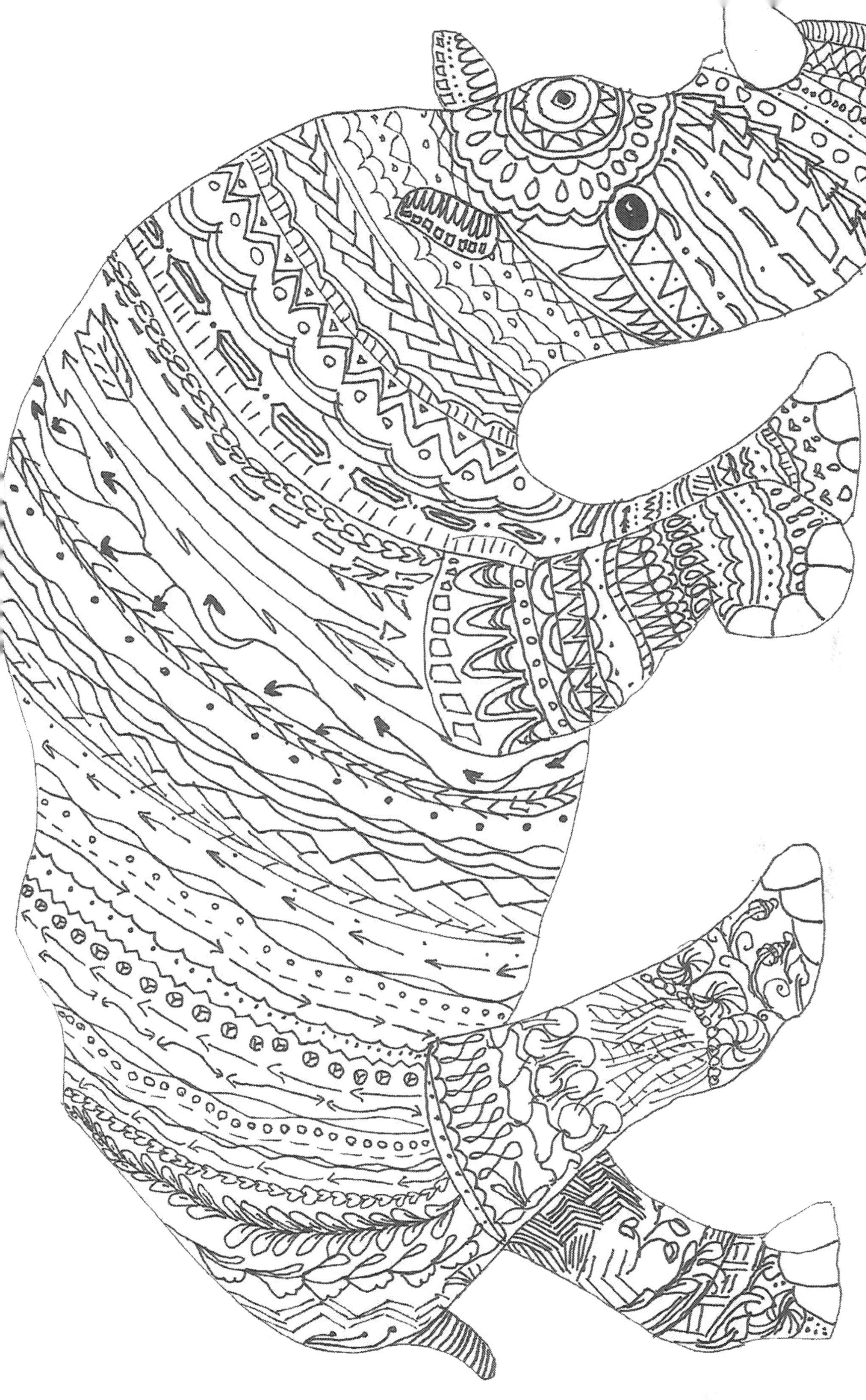

the waves are calling me...

Hook line & Sinker

Made in the USA
Columbia, SC
06 May 2025

57537053R00024